The Usborne HOLIDAY Activity Book

Written by
Rebecca Gilpin, James Maclaine
and Lucy Bowman

Designed and illustrated by
Erica Harrison, Jan McCafferty,
Tane Williams and Stella Baggott

Edited by Fiona Watt

You'll find the answers and solutions
to the puzzles on pages 92-96.

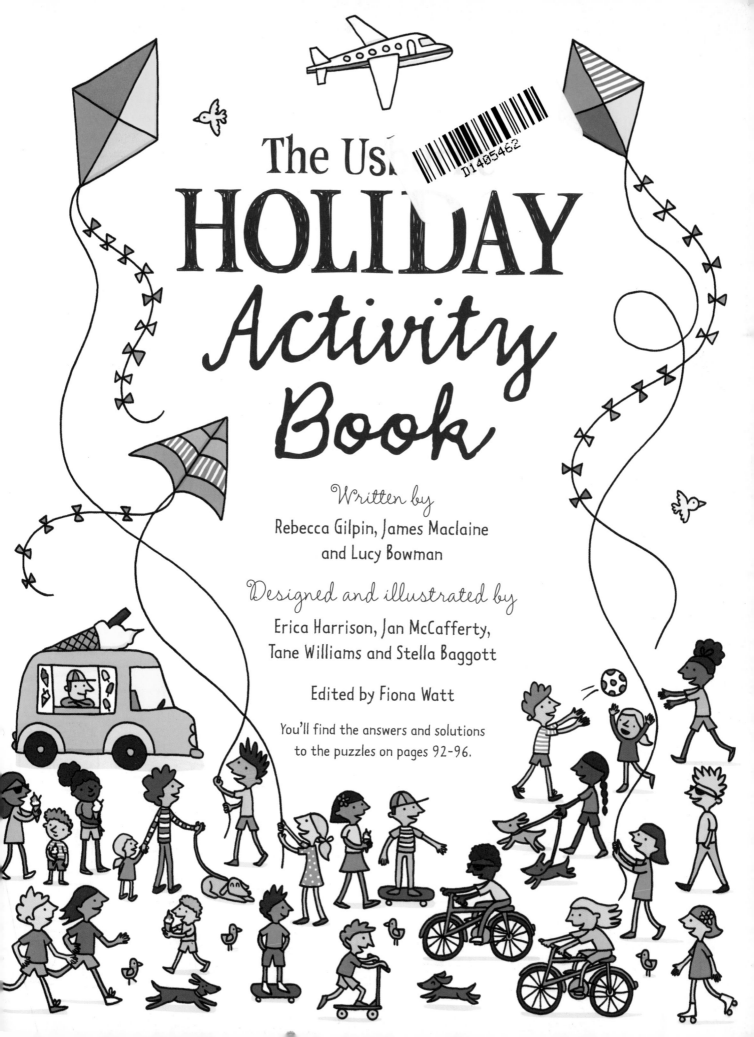

READY TO GO

SHADOW SHAPES

Luggage comes in all shapes and styles. Can you draw a line from each piece of luggage to its matching silhouette?

WHERE IN THE WORLD...

Play this game with one or more friends.

Mexico

Is it hot?

Yes.

Is it in Africa?

No.

Is it... Mexico?

Guessing a country counts as one of the questions.

Yes!

1. One person thinks of a country they'd like to visit.

2. Everyone else tries to guess it, using a total of 10 questions. The person thinking of it can only reply 'yes' or 'no'.

3. If someone guesses the correct country, they win. If no one's guessed it after 10 questions, the first person wins.

CLICKING CAMERAS

There are several pairs of cameras here, but one of them is on its own. Find it so that you can pack it for your trip.

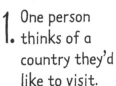
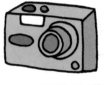

WHAT TO PACK?

Doodle lots of things you might pack to take away with you.

Doodle things you would pack for a trip to the beach.

Draw snow gear you might need on a skiing trip.

Doodle fun things you could take to keep you busy on a journey.

ONE MORE THING...

One final item needs to be packed into this bag. Which one is it?

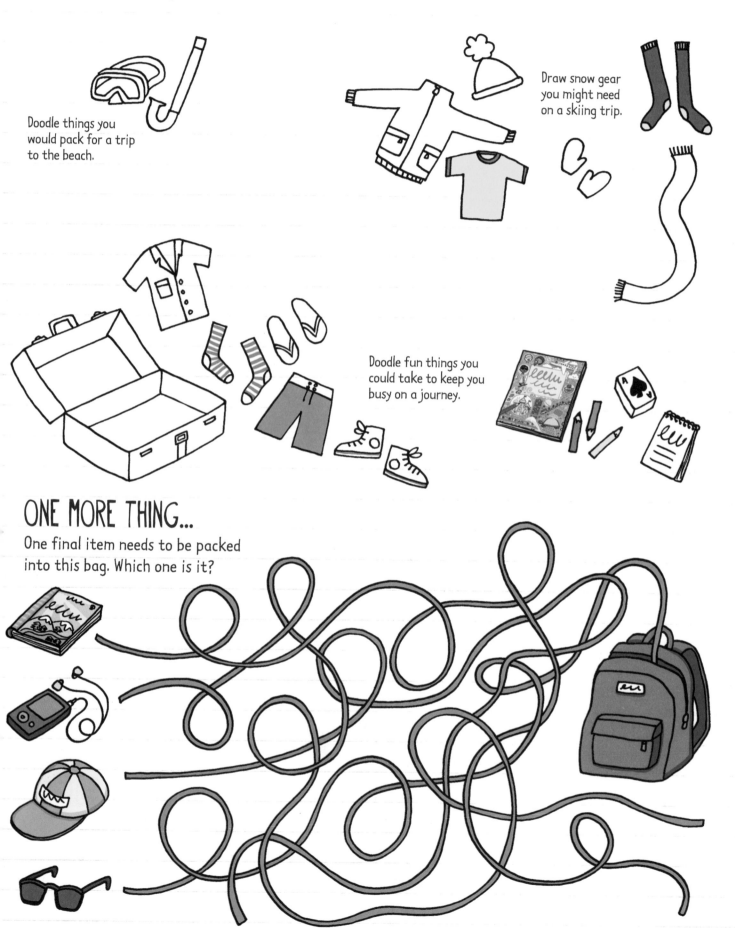

ALL ABOARD!

It's time for the ferry to sail away across the sea, but first the cars need to board and the cabins need to be prepared...

Doodle more seagulls in the sky.

Lining up

These cars are waiting to board. Follow the instructions to fill them all in.

☆ Make all the cars with luggage racks purple.
☆ All the cars between a red and a blue car need to be yellow.
☆ Then, fill in all the cars next to green cars in black pen or pencil.
☆ Make all the remaining cars orange.

Porthole puzzle

Each car you can see will need one cabin with a porthole, except for the cars with luggage racks, which will need two cabins. Figure out how many cabins will be occupied, then turn on their lights by filling them in with yellow pen or pencil.

DID YOU KNOW?

Big ships have a line painted on the side called a Plimsoll line. If it dips below the water, that means the ship is carrying too much weight.

5

BEACH FUN

OFF FOR A SWIM

Three friends want to go for a swim, but they have to find their way through all the people on the beach to reach the sea. Can you help them find the way?

START HERE

TANGLED STRINGS

The strings of these kites are all tangled up. Who is flying each kite?

A. . . . . . .   B. . . . . .   C. . . . . . .   D. . . . . . .

BUILDING SANDCASTLES

Doodle more sandcastles on this sand. Include...

 Flags

Doors and windows

Ramparts

Shells and pebbles

Here's one to start you off.

BEACH RACE

It's time for a running race, but there are lots of obstacles on the beach. Each kind of obstacle has a different number of points, and the winner is the runner with the fewest points. Add up each runner's points, to find out who wins the race:

OBSTACLE POINTS

Seashell – 1   Seaweed – 2

Spade – 3   Sandcastle – 4

Use this space for doing sums:

Runner. . . . . .wins, with. . . . . . . .points.

ICE CREAMS

Doodle

on, and colour in,
these ice creams
and ice lollies.

To draw an ice cream:

Draw a cone:

Draw lines going one way, then add lines going the other way:

Add some ice cream...
Like this: Or this:

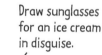

Doodle your own ice
creams in the gaps,
if you like.

Draw faces
on ice creams.

Draw sunglasses
for an ice cream
in disguise.

Add bright
sugar sprinkles.

Doodle a face on this
ice lolly, then fill it in.

Fill in cherries with
a red pen or pencil.

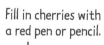

You could draw a toothy monster mouth.

Draw dribbles and a sad face for a melting ice cream.

Add dribbles of strawberry or chocolate sauce.

You could even draw a fly on an ice cream!

Draw two small curves for sleepy eyes.

Try using bright pens for outlines.

ROAD TRIP USA

ON THE ROAD

Doodle pictures on the road signs, to show the hazards that the car may encounter on its journey.

Doodle more spikes on the cacti.

FALLING LEAVES

It's Autumn, and the leaves are falling. Can you find two that are exactly the same?

AT THE DRIVE-IN

Five things don't belong in this old Western movie scene. Spot them and draw circles around them.

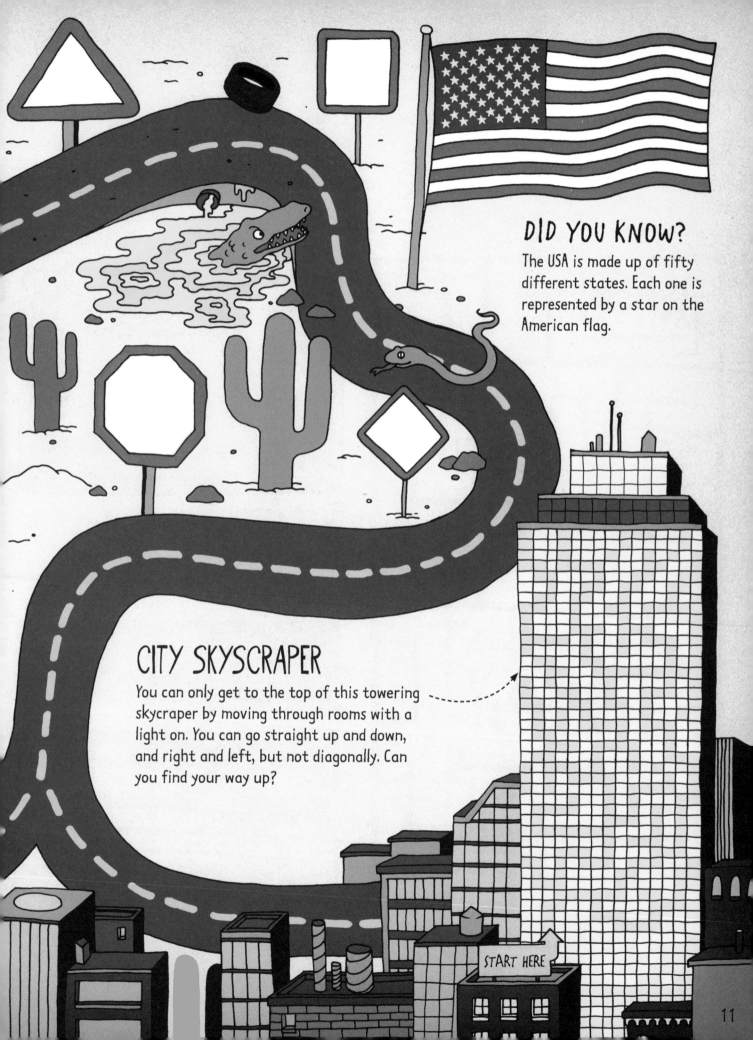

DID YOU KNOW?
The USA is made up of fifty different states. Each one is represented by a star on the American flag.

CITY SKYSCRAPER

You can only get to the top of this towering skycraper by moving through rooms with a light on. You can go straight up and down, and right and left, but not diagonally. Can you find your way up?

START HERE

DEPARTURES...

FLIGHT DASH

A passenger is late for his flight. Draw a line as quickly as you can, along the winding corridors, via the check-in desk and security, all the way to the gate. You mustn't bump into any of the walls with your pen!

CHECK-IN DESK

SECURITY

GATE 42

SUITCASE SEARCH

Can you find these items packed in the suitcase below? The words may be written vertically, horizontally, diagonally and even backwards.

CAMERA   SNORKEL   SUNGLASSES   SHORTS

BOOK   HAT   SHOES   TOWEL

S	E	S	S	A	L	G	N	U	S
L	K	H	M	C	R	E	O	H	R
E	O	O	B	A	H	E	R	A	E
K	O	R	P	M	S	N	H	T	M
R	B	T	L	E	W	O	T	A	A
O	A	S	O	R	E	M	S	K	C
N	U	H	O	A	D	H	L	M	E
S	S	U	N	C	O	O	B	A	R

DESTINATION UNKNOWN

There is something wrong with the flight departures board. Can you rearrange the letters to find out the five destination cities?

DEPARTURES						
O 9 3 5	MORE					
O 9 3 5						
O 9 4 5	SPIRA					
O 9 4 5						
O 9 5 O	TOOKY					
O 9 5 O						
1 O 1 O	WEN ROKY					
1 O 1 O						
1 O 1 5	JIBGINE					
1 O 1 5						

...AND ARRIVALS
FIND THE CASE

Can you find and circle the suitcase on the baggage carousel that matches the clues below?

The suitcase...
☆ has wheels
☆ is neither red nor green
☆ is missing its luggage label

PASSPORT CONTROL

The officials have spotted a badly-forged ID card. Can you spot and circle the five differences that led to their discovery?

MR. M. BIRD
02/03/1983
975831

MR. M. BIRD
03/02/1983
975831

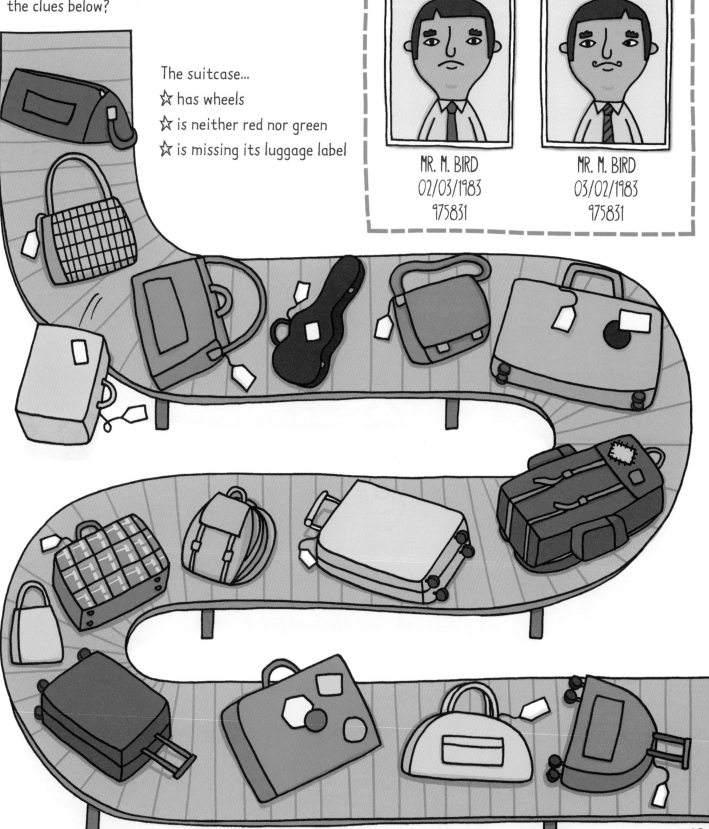

ON BOARD SHIP

DESTINATION DILEMMA

Write out the letters the ship passes as it sails towards the island, to find out where it's heading.

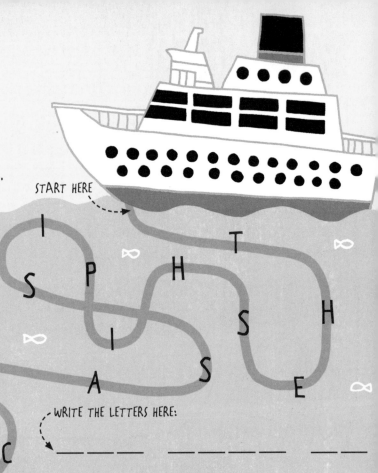

START HERE

N G I J A M L O I A T I C S P I A S H I S E T H

WRITE THE LETTERS HERE:

_ _ _ _ _ _ _ _ _

_ _ _ _ _ _ _ _

_ _ _ _ _ _

DID YOU KNOW?

There are different names for the front, back, left and right sides of a ship. They are:

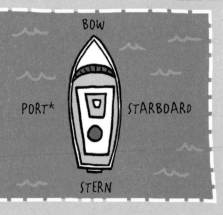

BOW

PORT*   STARBOARD

STERN

*If you stand on a ship facing towards its front, or bow, the port side is on your left.

HA HA HA!

Q: What's green and has four legs and two heads?

A: A couple of seasick tourists.

PUSH THE PUCKS

This shuffleboard player has to push his four pucks onto the triangular scoring area. Can you draw them in the correct sections to reach his score?

-10   7   8   10

Player's score = 12

Pucks

14

THE CAPTAIN'S TABLE

Use the food stickers from the sticker pages to set the table for dinner, following the captain's rules.

Rules

- Seafood on round dishes
- Meat on trays with handles
- Vegetarian food on plates with four edges
- Desserts on stands

GAMES ON THE GO

These games will keep you entertained when you're on the move – in a car, on a train or somewhere else...

ADVENTURE WORD GAME

Play this imagination game with as many people as you like.

Take turns to add five words at a time, and invent an exciting adventure together.

The famous explorer, Sir Charles...

...Blunderbuss, crept quietly past a...

...huge stone statue of a...

...dragon. It was surrounded by...

...thick foliage. Suddenly, he heard...

CAR PARTS

This is a game for two people. One person thinks of a word, and the other person has to try to identify it, before the first person has drawn a whole car.

1. Person 1 thinks of a word (it can be anything) and writes a short line for each letter on some paper:

Rocket

2. Person 2 guesses a letter that might be in the word.

E?

3. If it is in the word, Person 1 writes it in.

If not, they draw the first part of a car, then write the letter and draw a line through it.

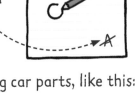

4. They both continue in the same way, guessing letters, and filling in letters or adding car parts, like this:

Start with one wheel...

Add the front and back of the car...

Draw windows...

...and add a driver.

Person 2 can guess a whole word instead of a letter, but if it's wrong, Person 1 adds another car part.
Person 2 wins if the word is complete before the car is finished. Person 1 wins if the car is finished first.

You can play the game in this space.

16

TRAIN TRIP

In this memory game, take turns to add something to the list, and see how many things you can remember in a row:

On this train, there's... a suitcase.

On this train, there's... a suitcase and a man in a hat.

On this train, there's... a suitcase, a man in a hat and a black dog.

On this train, there's... a suitcase, a man in a hat, a black dog and a book.

If you're on a plane, you could play this with things that you might find on a plane instead.

AMERICA, BRAZIL, CROATIA...

In this game, take turns to think of a country that begins with each letter of the alphabet. Start with the letter A, then B and so on:

America

Brazil

Croatia

Some letters may be too hard, so before you start, agree which ones you're going to leave out.

You can also play this game with kinds of animals, kinds of food, or even with no theme at all.

CAN'T SEE IT ANYWHERE

In this imagination game, only say things that you CAN'T see...

1. One person starts by thinking of something that they can't see. They say "I can't see..." then give two clues: the kind of thing it is (in this example, an animal) and its first letter (T):

I can't see... an animal that starts with a T.

2. The other person tries to guess what it is they're thinking of:

Turtle?

3. If they guess correctly, it's their turn to think of something new. If they can't guess it, the first person has another turn.

Tiger?

Yes!

ISLAND-HOPPING
VILLAGE VISIT

It's a busy day in this fishing village – can you spot and circle the following?:

☆ two men in white hats
☆ three people with dogs
☆ a man taking a photograph
☆ eight birds
☆ six cats
☆ two boys eating ice cream
☆ an artist painting a picture

FISHING PUZZLE

Juan, Noah and Alex have had a fun day out fishing, but their fish are all mixed together. How many did each boy catch?

I caught small fish...

I caught medium-sized fish...

...and I caught BIG fish!

Juan ....   Noah ....   Alex ....

Fill in the fish as you count them, using a different pen for each size.

ISLAND NAMES

See if you can sort out these jumbled-up island names:

IABL

....

ZIABI

....

ETREC

....

BRODSABA

....

SUMMER SALAD

You'll find salads similar to this on Greek islands. To make enough salad for four people, you'll need:

Slice me!
half a cucumber

Cut us in half...
450g (1lb) small tomatoes

...and slice me finely!
1 red onion

Cut me into cubes.
200g (7oz) of feta or semi-hard cheese

We can be black...   ...or green!
several pitted olives

For a dressing, you'll need:

2 tablespoons of olive oil

Squeeze me!
half a lemon

Peel me and crush me!
1 small clove of garlic

a pinch of salt and ground black pepper

1. Mix the salad ingredients in a large bowl.

2. Mix the dressing ingredients in a mug.

Use a fork.

3. Drizzle the dressing over the salad and mix it in. Serve the salad straightaway.

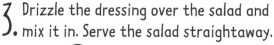
Serve the salad with fresh crusty bread.

At the carnival

Fantastic fireworks

Which of these fireworks isn't part of a matching pair? Colour that one in, then colour in the others.

Carnival parade

It's carnival time and the streets are filled with people celebrating. There are lots of things for you to spot...

Can you find seven blue lanterns?

Can you spot two red noses?

Mysterious masks

Lots of people at carnivals wear masks – here's how to make one:

1. Draw around sunglasses on thin cardboard...

Add a mask shape...

...and shapes for eye holes.

2. Cut out the mask...

...and each eye hole.

3. Tape a drinking straw to the back of the mask.

4. Now decorate your mask...

Feathers

Sequins

Glitter

Ribbon

Find a hat decorated with a flower.

There are three jugglers – can you see them all?

Holiday hotel

Enjoy your stay... and see if you can solve the puzzles in all the rooms in this hotel.

What's different?

The guests staying in Room 30 have arrived, but no one is in Room 29 yet. Draw a circle around five things that are different in Room 30.

Dining room dilemma

The tables in the dining room need setting with a glass, plate, knife, fork and spoon at each place setting. How many settings can be made?

Menu code

There are lots of delicious things on today's menu – but there's also something hidden here... Can you see a message in the menu?

ANSWER:..........

today's specials

tomaTo soup
Ham and mElon
pRawn cocktail
***
roast bEef
spaghettI bologneSe
vegetAble risotto
Fish curry
***
Lemon and strawberrY swIrl
cocoNuT clusters
cHEeSecake
chOcolate fUdge Pudding

Up on the roof

Doodle more plants in the pots.

Colour in the tiles

Fill in the rest of the tiles in the same pattern.

Bathroom sudoku

Draw pictures of these four bathroom objects in the grid.

Every row and column must have one picture of each object.

THE SAFFRON HOTEL

How many words can you find in the hotel name above? For each word, only use each letter the number of times it appears. Write your words on the door.

Elevator race

These elevators are on the first floor, and have different stops to make. Each time an elevator moves to a new floor, it takes three seconds. Each time an elevator stops at a floor, it takes an additional six seconds. If no more buttons are pressed, which elevator will finish its journey first?

A.   B.   C.

Do your sums here:

SUMMER GARDEN

LOST IN A MAZE

This boy has wandered deep into a maze and is now lost.
Can you help him find his way out?

BUG SEARCH

This garden is filled with bugs hiding among the plants. How many of each
of the following can you spot? Colour them in as you go to help you count.
Then, colour the rest of the picture.

CATERPILLARS.......... BUTTERFLIES..........

BEETLES.......... BEES..........

SPIDERS..........

GARDEN BALL GAME

1. Everyone stands in a circle, with one person holding a ball.

2. She calls out the name of a plant or flower, then throws the ball to someone else.

TULIP

3. That person must call out the name of a different plant or flower, before catching the ball.

FERN

4. If someone misses the ball, doesn't call out in time, or repeats a plant or flower name, they are out.

DAFFODIL

TULI...OOPS!

5. The last person left wins.

MAKE THE BED

Work out how many flowers and plants should fill the empty bed, then draw them.

Doodle more flowers and bugs.

25

GALLERY GAZING

Put the finishing touches to this gallery by completing the activities on these pages.

STICK PEOPLE
Doodle more people in this picture.

FACE IT
Turn this shape into a portrait.

PAINTING PATTERNS
Fill in the shapes with different colours.

PICTURE IMPERFECT
The portrait on the top right is a forgery. Can you spot seven missing details and draw them in?

WALK THE LINE
Doodle a pattern to fill the frame, trying not to take your pen off the paper.

SQUARED
Find out how many squares there are in this picture by drawing over each one with different coloured pens.

Answer: ....

THEME PARK FUN
ROLLERCOASTER RIDE

This ride is the fastest in the park. Give the passengers waving arms, doodle wind-swept hair on their heads, and draw their excited faces.

SUPER SPINNER

The pictures on this big wheel form a pattern. Can you draw on the final picture?

WILD WATER

These water rings have sums painted on their sides. The person riding the ring with the biggest answer will get the wettest! Fill in the answers to figure out who it will be.

$25 - 8 =$

$14 + 6 =$

$27 - 11 =$

$7 + 12 =$

BRILLIANT BALLOONS

One of these balloons is going to pop!
Follow the instructions below until
there is just one balloon left, then
draw a bird about to pop it.

Count these objects in the
theme park, then cross out
those numbers on the balloons:

☆ Water rings
☆ Ice cubes
☆ Lightning bolts
☆ Birds
☆ Trees
☆ Pink goldfish
☆ Arrows

Win a prize

To win this game, spot which prize is
the odd one out on each row.

Island worlds

Using your imagination (and a pen), transform these islands into island worlds, and fill the seas with ships and sea creatures...

Add houses, trees, animals and birds on the islands.

Doodle squirting whales and fearsome sharks in the sea.

Draw more birds flying in the sky.

Add ships, sailing from island to island.

You could even draw a submarine on a secret mission...

HOLIDAYING AT HOME
FRIENDS' VISIT

Which two friends are going to visit Nick?

James

Lucy

Tilly

Nick's house

Armand

BARBECUE PRANKS

Someone's been playing some silly pranks at this barbecue. Spot and circle six things that don't seem right:

SPOT THE SPOONS

Find the two spoons and colour them in:

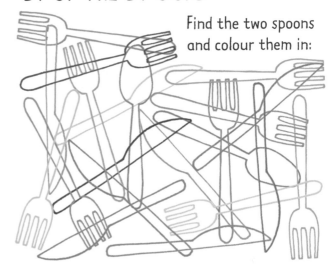

CUPCAKE MONSTERS

Make mini cupcakes, then decorate them with monster faces. First, heat your oven to 180°C, 350°F or gas mark 4.

To make 24 cupcakes, you will need:

And for the icing:

Crack me!

Sieve me!

Sieve me!

1 medium egg, broken into a mug

50g (2oz) self-raising flour

40g (1½oz) soft margarine

40g (1½oz) caster sugar

24 small paper cases, on a baking tray

50g (2oz) icing sugar

about a tablespoon of water

1. Put the cupcake ingredients into a large bowl and stir them well, until the mixture is smooth and creamy.

2. Using a teaspoon, half-fill each paper case with the mixture.

3. Bake the cupcakes for about 12 minutes, then put them onto a wire rack to cool.

4. Mix the icing sugar and water in a small bowl. Add a drop or two of food colouring, if you like.

5. When the cupcakes are cool, blob some icing on each one. Spread it out with the back of a teaspoon.

6. Make your cupcakes into monsters, using little sweets, sugar sprinkles and writing icing. Here are some ideas:

The pupils on my eyes are writing icing.

Press on a jelly sweet for a nose.

Press on sweets for eyes.

My spots are writing icing.

My toothy mouth is writing icing too.

You could scatter sugar sprinkles onto the icing.

Break a chocolate button in half for pointed ears.

DIVING FOR TREASURE

These divers have heard that there's amazing treasure inside the wreck of 'The Valiant'. They need to swim to the room that's filled with treasure, avoiding the dangerous sea creatures lurking inside the ship. Can you find a safe route for them to take?

DANGER!
Avoid these sea creatures:

JELLYFISH: painful stinging tentacles.

STINGRAY: poisonous spine on tail, may lash out to protect itself.

LIONFISH: bright poisonous spines.

STONEFISH: lies still, deadly poisonous.

MORAY EEL: may bite if it feels threatened.

ELEPHANTS AND SPICES

BUSY VILLAGE

Look closely at this busy scene and count all the things that you need to solve the sums below.

First solve sums [A], [B] and [C], then use the answers to work out the total at the bottom:

[A] Houses ...... ÷ Elephants ...... = ...

[B] Cows ...... x Cats ...... = ...

[C] Dogs ...... ÷ Bicycles ...... = ...

Now solve these sums to find out the total:

Answer [B] ...... ÷ Answer [C] ...... = ...

+ Answer [A] ...... = ... – Cows ......

= TOTAL ......

SPICE SHOP

Can you decipher the labels on these spices?

A	B	C	D	E	F	G	H	I	J	K	L	M	N	O	P	Q	R	S	T	U	V	W	X	Y	Z

DOTTY PALACE

Join the dots from 1 to 93, to reveal the hidden palace:

FIND THE GEM

Can you find one blue sapphire amongst these gems?

ELEPHANTS' DAY OUT

At some festivals and other special occasions, people dress elephants in fabrics and sometimes paint them with patterns. Decorate these elephants, using bright colours:

FUN WITH FRIENDS

DICE DOGS

Players take turns rolling a dice and drawing the part of a dog that corresponds to the number rolled.

Each player must throw a...

☆ 6 for the dog's body
☆ 5 for each ear
☆ 4 for each eye
☆ 3 for each leg
☆ 2 for its tail
☆ 1 for its head

You must draw its body first, and then its head (so you need to throw a 6 to start, then a 1). Then, you can draw the other parts in any order.

The winner is the first person to draw a complete dog.

BEE TAKEAWAY

This is a two-player game. When it's your turn, cross out as many bees as you like - but only from one of the four rows. The winner is the person who forces the loser to cross out the last remaining bee.

To play this game again, draw four more rows of bees, or four rows of circles, on some paper.

FUNNY FIGURES

Each person will need a pen and a strip of paper.

1. First draw a head and neck.

2. Fold the paper over, and pass it to someone else.

Make sure you can see the end of the neck.

3. Then, draw a body and arms.

4. Fold the paper over again, and pass it on.

Leave the end of the body showing

5. Then, draw legs.

6. Fold the paper and pass it on.

Leave the ankles showing.

7. Then, draw the feet.

8. Fold the paper and pass it on.

9. Unfold each piece of paper to reveal what everyone's drawn.

PAPER SPINNERS

For each spinner, you'll need: a 5 x 20cm (2 x 8in) strip of paper and a paperclip.

1. Draw a line down the middle of the paper...

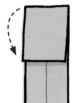

...and fold down the top third.

2. Unfold it and cut down the line to the fold.

Then, draw a line a little way below the fold.

3. Make two marks halfway between each edge and the middle.

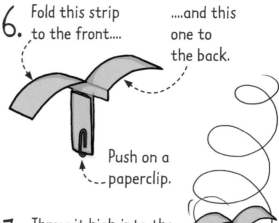

Cut up to these marks.

4. Fold in both edges so that they meet in the middle.

5. Fold up the bottom edge to this line.

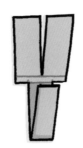

6. Fold this strip to the front.... ....and this one to the back.

Push on a paperclip.

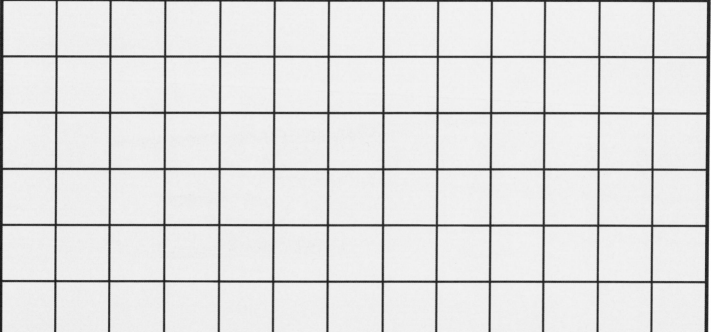

7. Throw it high into the air, and see it spin down to the ground.

GRID LOCKED

Take turns placing the shape stickers from the sticker pages onto this grid. The last person who can fit a sticker on the grid is the winner.

Air show

Using the stickers from the sticker pages, add hot-air balloons, helicopters and birds to the sky. Then, draw a line to show the route that the stunt plane will take across the sky.

ON THE SLOPES
WHICH WAY DOWN?

Can you guide the snowboarder down to the bottom of the mountain? Watch out for trees, snowdrifts and skiers.

Doodle

different designs on the snowboards, then colour them in.

NAME EVERY MOUNTAIN

The names of four famous mountains can be found on the mountains below. Starting at the top of each mountain, find its name by adding the correct letter or set of letters from each layer.

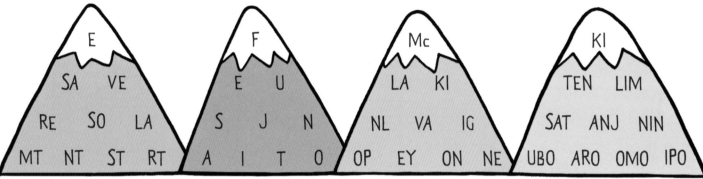

Write the names here:

....

ODD SKIER OUT

Can you spot and circle what's different about each of these skiers?

SORT THE SKIS

Link each pair of skis, then circle the odd ski.

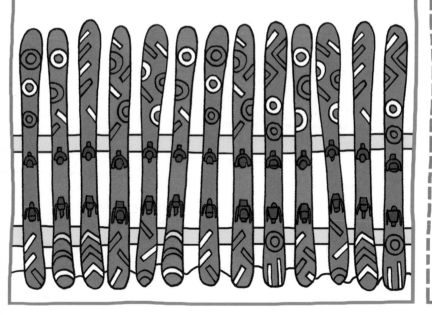

SNOWED OUT

Some snowballs are covering the adding and taking away symbols in these sums. Add the symbols, to arrive at the correct answers.

$12 \bigcirc 5 \bigcirc 3 = 10$

$14 \bigcirc 2 \bigcirc 1 = 11$

$90 \bigcirc 40 \bigcirc 30 = 80$

$7 \bigcirc 3 \bigcirc 2 \bigcirc 4 = 8$

In the museum

It's a busy day in the museum. Lots of people have come to visit. Can you spot and circle the items listed on these pages?

☆ three cameras

☆ five museum leaflets

☆ three people wearing hats

☆ two snakes

☆ a visitor who's fallen asleep

44

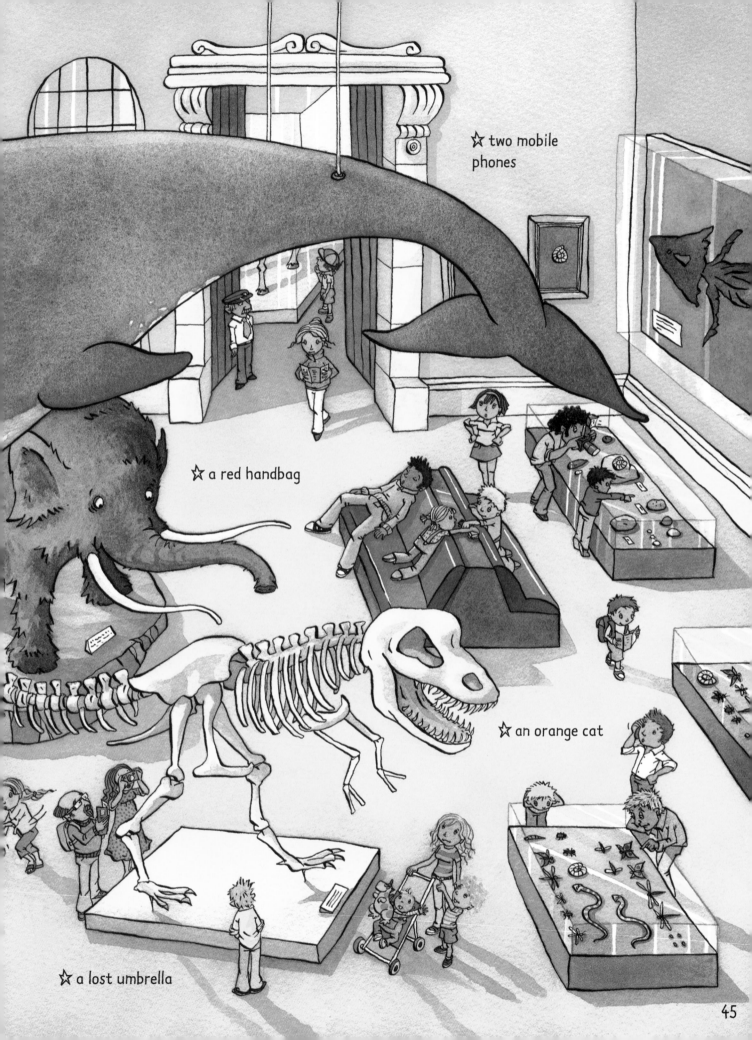

☆ two mobile phones

☆ a red handbag

☆ an orange cat

☆ a lost umbrella

45

CASTLE DAY OUT

Take a tour around this castle and its different activities.

LONG GALLERY

Complete these family portraits.

DID YOU KNOW?

In some castles, you can still see the original toilet, or garderobe, used in medieval times. It was often just a hole in the floor located above the moat.

ARMOURY

This shield is symmetrical. When you divide it in half with a straight line, each half is an exact reflection of the other.

A.

B.

C.

D.

Circle the other symmetrical shields.

These four suits of armour aren't quite the same. Can you spot and circle the difference in each one?

LIBRARY

Find and circle these three groups of books on the library shelves.

1.
2.
3.

BANQUETING HALL

The number of candles on each stand follows a pattern from left to right. Work it out and draw in the missing candles.

COURTYARD

Can you circle five strange details in this jousting re-enactment?

Sunshine

Doodle different faces on these suns.

Draw a hat.

Add some sunglasses.

Draw half circles for eyes on a very happy face.

Give some suns rosy cheeks.

Showers

Draw a different face on each cloud and raindrop.

Try drawing a sleepy face.

Draw in more raindrops.

Add zigzags for lightning.

CAMPING OUT

Get ready for the great outdoors with these camping puzzles and activities.

Doodle leaves on the trees.

PITCH THE TENTS

Read the sign, then stick the tents from the sticker pages in the correct order around the camp fire.

Tent Rules

☆ Red is between green and orange.
☆ Blue is furthest to the left.
☆ Blue is next to orange.
☆ Yellow is next to green.

KNOW YOUR KNOTS

Here are some knots you might find useful if you were to go camping. Try tying them with some rope or string.

CLOVE HITCH
This knot's good for tying something to a post.

Make two loops.

Place this loop...

...over the other.

Slip both loops over a post.

Pull both ends of the rope tightly.

HEAVING LINE BEND
This knot ties together a thin rope and a thick one.

Weave the thin rope under the thick one...

...wrap it around...

...and pull it down through.

SLING
Use this knot to carry a bucket that's missing its handle.

Place the bucket on the string.

Tie the ends of the string over the bucket.

Pull the loop apart and slip it over the bucket.

Tighten the loop around the bucket.

Tie the ends to make a handle.

MARSHMALLOW SEQUENCE

The numbers on each of these sticks of marshmallows follow a different sequence. Write in the missing numbers:

3 — 9 — 12

2 — 4 — 16

35 — 21 — 7

PACK THE BACKPACK

The words on this packing list are missing their vowels: A, E, I, O, U. Can you guess what they should be and write them below?

LIST
1. CLTHS
2. FLSK
3. TRCH
4. WTR BTTL
5. SLPNG BG

1. _____
2. _____
3. _____
4. _____ _____
5. _____ _____

DESERT DAY OUT

HOT HIKERS

These hikers are looking forward to a cool drink. Can you guide them through the rocky landscape to the roadside café?

OUCH!

A cowboy has been thrown from his horse and landed on some cacti, each of which started off with 20 spines. Which ones did he land on, and how many spines did he get from each one? Circle each cactus he landed on.

Spines missing: A..... B..... C..... D..... E.....

TRUE OR FALSE?

Circle each correct answer.

1. Deserts are always hot.   TRUE / FALSE

2. Sand dunes move.   TRUE / FALSE

3. Flowers can grow in deserts.   TRUE / FALSE

4. All deserts are sandy.   TRUE / FALSE

5. Many desert animals only come out at night.   TRUE / FALSE

ROCKY WORDS

Find these words hidden in the rock – they may be going up, down, across and even backwards:

CACTUS

DESERT

DRY

HOT

INSECTS

ROCKS

SAND

SUN

```
D N T R E S E D
I H E O G I C M E O
N O L R S A D L A C
C T Y S T O I N S K
M I C A C T U S A N
R D X S E H L B X S
O N E H S R A V R U
L A F B N E P A C N
D S U L I W D R Y C
H R O C K S E G
```

CANYON CLIMB

Which way should this climber go up the rock face? There are lots of ledges for him to climb on. Each time he moves, the next ledge needs to be two squares up and one square to the left or right.

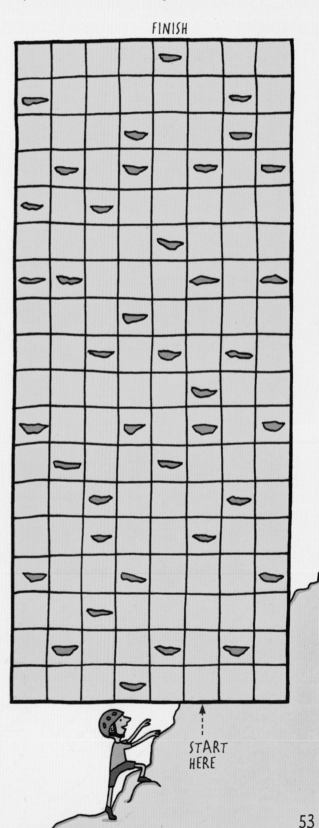

FINISH

START HERE

HUNGRY ARMADILLO

Which trail should this armadillo follow, to have a feast of juicy ants?

A.   B.   C.   D.

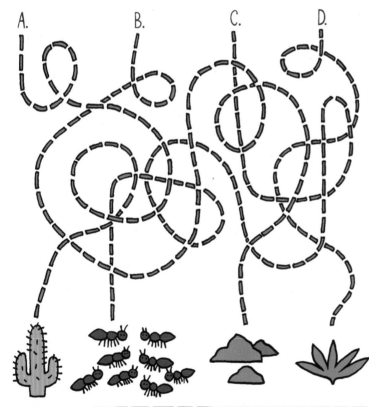

Boredom busters

Code-named creatures

Match the word puzzles below with these codes.
Then, see if you can work out...

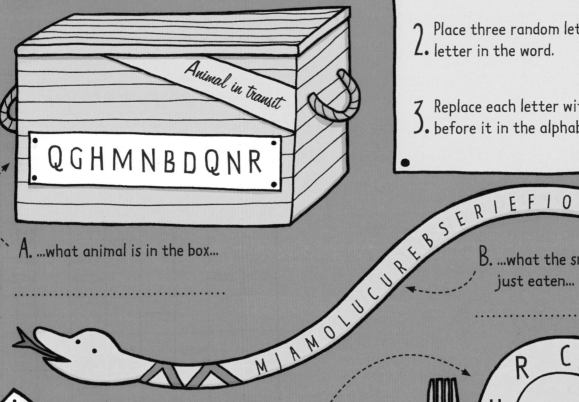

A. ...what animal is in the box...

....

B. ...what the snake has
just eaten...

....

C. ...and what kind of insect
has run across this plate?

....

CODES

1. Write the letters in a circle, so that every other letter spells out the word, as you go round and round clockwise starting at '12 o'clock'.

   Puzzle: ....

2. Place three random letters after every letter in the word.

   Puzzle: ....

3. Replace each letter with the letter before it in the alphabet.

   Puzzle: ....

Animal in transit

QGHMNBDQNR

MIAMOLUCUREBSERIEFIO

R C
H   O
O
K   A
C C

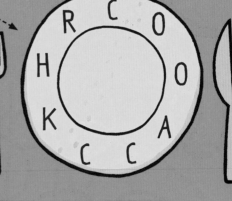

Pattern problem

Can you colour in this pattern
with three different pens,
so that no two birds the
same colour are next
to each other?

Colour squares

The nine small squares that make up the big square below each stand for a number according to their colour. Looking at the totals of each row and column, can you discover what number the different colours represent?

Then, write in the totals for each row or column that makes up this shape.

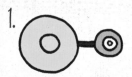
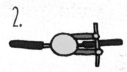
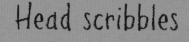 = ...

18
10
8

12 10 14

= ....

= ....

= ....

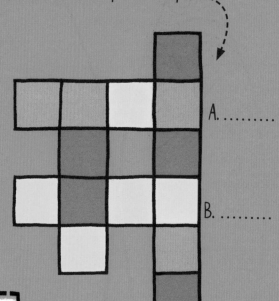

A. ....

B. ....

C. ....

D. ....

From above

What's happening in each of these pictures? Clue: they're bird's-eye views.

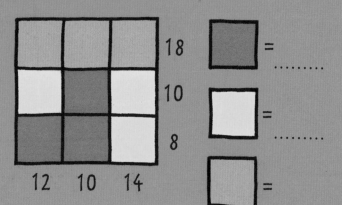

1.   2.   3.

Head scribbles

Turn these shapes into faces. - - - - -

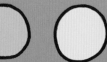

Guess how?

I have seven friends and a box of seven chocolates. How can I give each of my friends a chocolate and still have one left in the box?

SURF'S UP!

Brighten up these surfboards and surfer clothes:

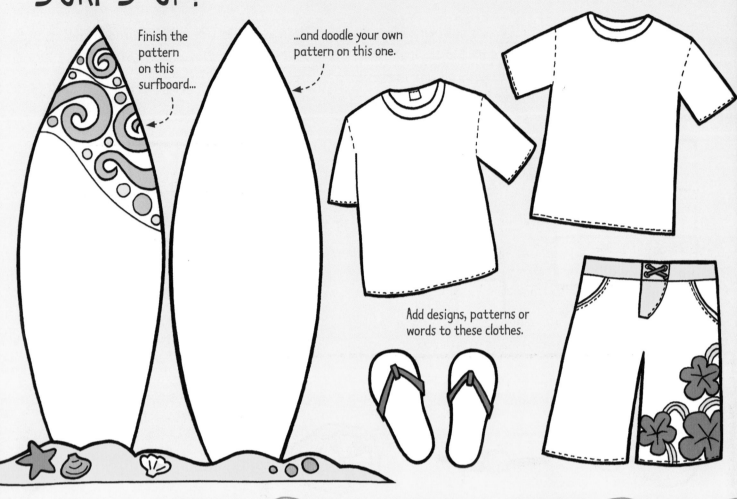

Finish the pattern on this surfboard...

...and doodle your own pattern on this one.

Add designs, patterns or words to these clothes.

OUT ON THE WAVES

Draw a windsurfer

Draw a board, a mast and a sail...

...then add a windsurfer.

Doodle more people windsurfing and enjoying other water sports.

VAN-TASTIC

At some surfing beaches, there are lots of brightly-coloured camper vans.

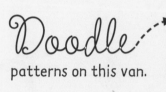

patterns on this van.

See how many words you can find in the word –

WINDSURFERS

Each time, only use each letter the number of times that it appears in the word.

Write your words in the space.

SURFER TALK

Surfing has a language of its own. Here are some surfing words:

☆ Set - group of waves.
☆ Lip - crest of a breaking wave.
☆ Barrel - space inside the curve of a breaking wave.
☆ Glassy - windless conditions, when the sea's surface is very smooth.
☆ Rail - edge (side) of a surfboard.
☆ Wipe-out - when someone falls off a surfboard as they're surfing a wave.

Japanese journey

Sightseeing

Your tour of Japan is about to begin – you just need to find your guide. Which square is she in?

☆ She's not in a square with water in it.

☆ She is in a square next to a building.

☆ She can see a tree in a square next to her.

☆ She doesn't like mountains.

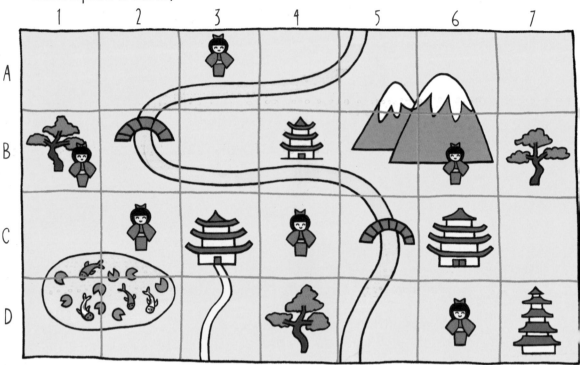

Lucky cats

These cat statues bring good luck to their owners, but one is the odd one out – can you spot it?

Sushi sequence

These sushi dishes have been arranged in a pattern. Which dish comes next? A, B or C?

A.   B.   C.

Super sushi

Draw pictures of the four different sushi pieces in this grid.

Every row and column must have one picture of each kind of sushi.

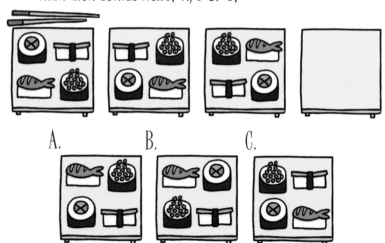

Kirigami flowers

Kirigami is the art of folding and cutting paper to make unusual shapes. To make your own, fold a square of paper...

1. once... twice... three times.

2. Draw shapes on the paper, like this.

3. Cut them out.

4. Open it up.

Count the cherry blossoms

Fill them in as you go.

Write the total here:

....

Lily pond

Can you find a safe path for this frog across the lily pond?

Finish over this side

Avoid carp...

...and broken lilypads.

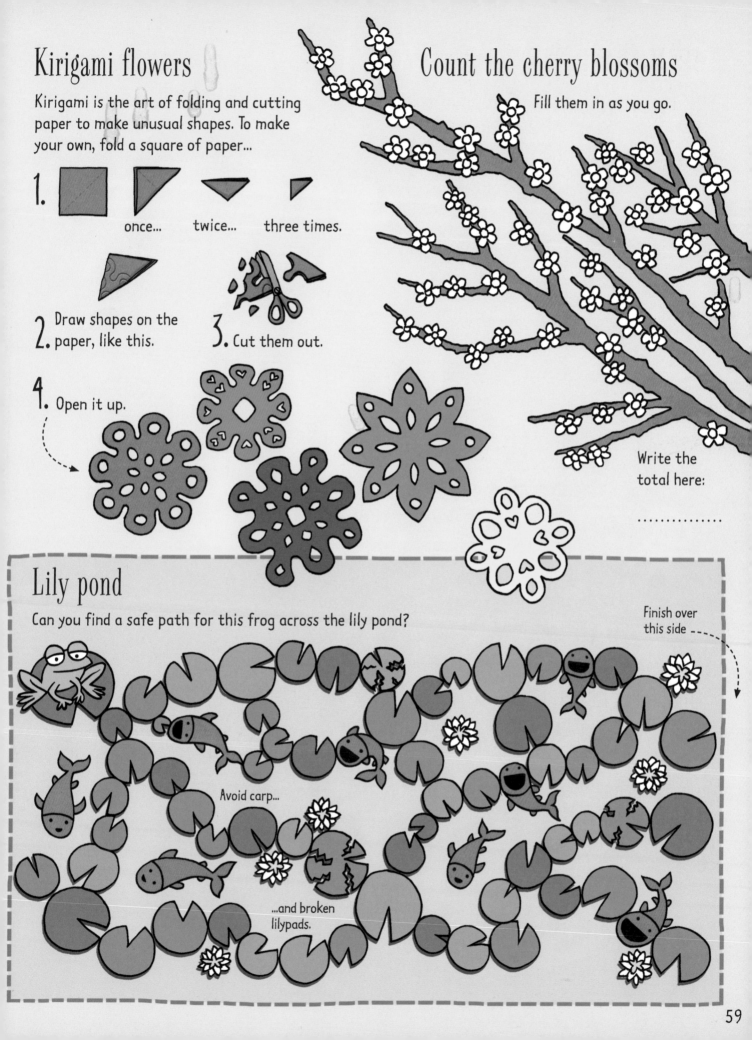

OUT OF THIS WORLD

Just imagine if you could holiday in space...
On these pages, you can be a space tourist,
visiting planets and solving puzzles. Press on
space stickers from the sticker pages, too.

Join each pair of space tourists
with a line. Circle the odd one
out. (Clue: have a good look at
their spacesuits.)

Can you help this boy get
back to his rocket ship?

TRUE OR FALSE?

There's no wind or rain on
the Moon, so the footprints
of the astronauts who
landed on the Moon are
still there.

These people want to go driving in space buggies. How many buggies can you make from the parts on this planet, and will there be enough buggies for them all?

Number of buggies: ....
Are there enough? ....

This is what a buggy looks like when it's built.

People on this planet have written a coded message. First, crack the code:

1. 2. 3. 4. 5
A _ _ _ E
6. 7. 8 . 9. 10. 11. 12. 13. 14
H _ _ _ _ _ _ _ _
15. 16. 17. 18. 19. 20. 21. 22. 23. 24. 25. 26
R _ T _ _ _ _ _ _ _ _ _

Then, translate their message:
5. 1. 18. 20. 8   12. 15. 15. 11. 19
_ _ _ _ _   _ _ _ _ _

7. 18. 5. 1. 20   6. 18. 15. 13
_ _ _ _ _   _ _ _ _

8. 5. 18. 5 !
_ _ _ _ !

How many times can you find the word 'STAR' here? It could be going vertically or horizontally, or maybe backwards.

```
S R S A T
R T S T A R A
R A S T R T A S R
S A S T A A S T R A R
T R T A T S R A T T A
R A T S A T A T S R S
S T A A R A S T A A T
A R T R T R A S A T S
S T A S T R S T S
S T A R T A S
A R T S R
```

CHILLING OUT
SNOW MYSTERY

It has snowed overnight and everything is covered with a blanket of snow. Which of these pictures shows the scene before it snowed?

RUNAWAY REINDEER

Some of these reindeer have run so fast that they've lost their antlers! Doodle antlers on the reindeer that don't have any.

FLAG-FINDER

Looking at the clues below, can you work out which flag belongs to each country?

☆ The Swedish flag has some blue on it.
☆ The Danish flag has a white cross on it.
☆ The Norwegian flag has a blue cross on it.
☆ The Finnish flag has a white background.

A.   B.

C.   D.

SWEDEN
(Swedish) ....

FINLAND
(Finnish) ....

NORWAY
(Norwegian) ....

DENMARK
(Danish) ....

DID YOU KNOW?

In some places in or near the Arctic Circle, there are hotels made almost entirely from ice. Each Spring, they melt, and have to be built again in the Winter.

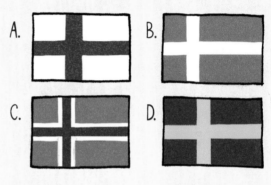

ISLAND CRUISE

The Moonstar is ready to set sail...
Following the instructions below,
draw the ship's route on the chart.
How many islands does it visit in
total, and which island is the
final destination in the cruise?

R R D L L D L D D R D R R R R
U L U U U R R R R D R D D R
(D = down, U = up, L = left, R = right)

TIP: For the Moonstar to 'visit' an island,
it just has to go into a square that
contains a part of that island.

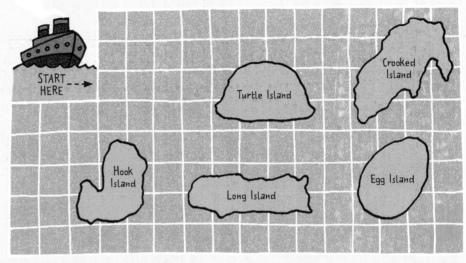

START HERE - - - ➔

Turtle Island

Crooked Island

Hook Island

Long Island

Egg Island

Number of islands visited: ....   Destination: ....

OPEN SANDWICHES

To make an open sandwich, you'll need:

a slice
of bread

 a little
butter

sandwich toppings (whatever you like best)
– here are some ideas:

salami

tomato slices

lettuce

thinly-sliced
cheese

ham

tuna mixed with
mayonnaise

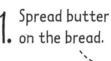

1. Spread butter
on the bread.

2. Layer your toppings on top of the bread.
Eat the sandwich with a knife and fork.

WATER PARK

Which is fastest?

One of these slides is quicker to go down than the other two. Work out the sums on each slide, then add the totals together – the slide with the highest total is the fastest.

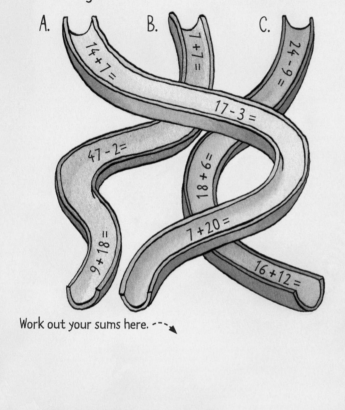

A.

14 + 7 =

B.

7 + 7 =

C.

24 − 9 =

17 − 3 =

47 − 2 =

18 + 6 =

9 + 18 =

7 + 20 =

16 + 12 =

Work out your sums here. - - ->

Swimmers

These swimmers all have stripy costumes – but which is the odd one out and why?

Super slides

This girl wants to go on a slide, but she's having trouble choosing. Which slide should she pick?

☆ She's afraid of the dark.　　☆ She wants something to sit on.　　☆ She doesn't like going too slowly.

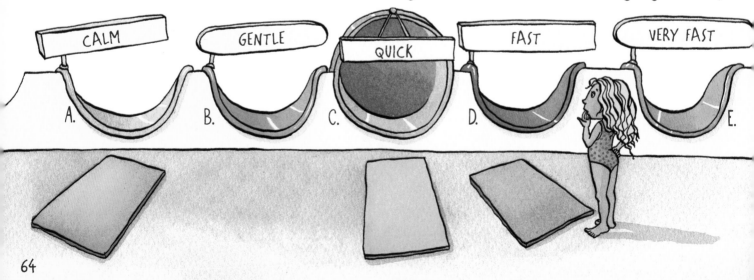

CALM　　GENTLE　　QUICK　　FAST　　VERY FAST

A.　　B.　　C.　　D.　　E.

Slide finds

The park is packed with people swimming, splashing and having fun! There are lots of things to spot...

☆ four people wearing yellow swimsuits
☆ a dropped ice cream
☆ four people wearing sunglasses
☆ a lady in a red hat

☆ eight palm trees
☆ three sun umbrellas
☆ a brown bird
☆ ten red flowers

IN THE WILDS

Test out your survival skills in the wilderness with these puzzles.

TRACKING DOWN

Draw a line to link each animal and the track it leaves in the mud.

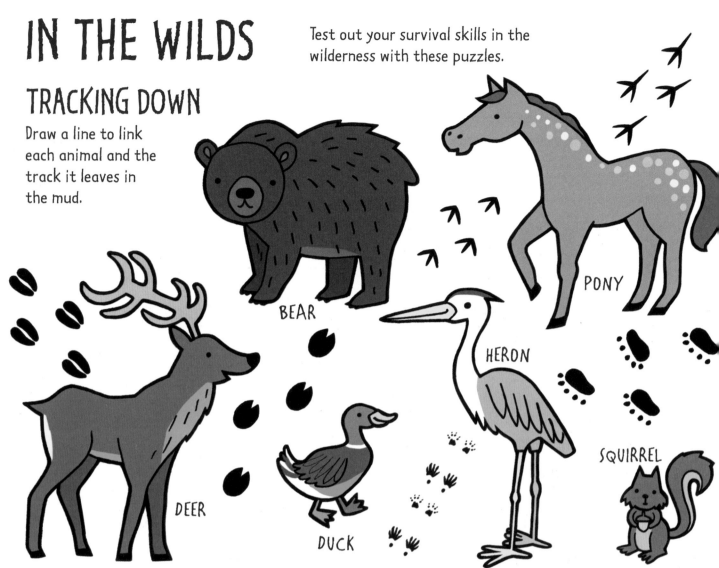

BEAR

PONY

DEER

HERON

DUCK

SQUIRREL

PICTURE PLOTTING

Plot out the points with dots on the grid. Draw a line from each dot to the next, in the order they appear. Then, colour the picture the lines make.

Find this number on the top row...

...and this number on the side column...

...then draw a dot where a line from the top number and a line from the side number would meet.

(i) 4,14 (ii) 5,14 (iii) 7,12 (iv) 7,9
(v) 8,8 (vi) 11,8 (vii) 13,10 (viii) 13,7
(ix) 9,3 (x) 4,3 (xi) 3,5 (xii) 3,8 (xiii) 5,10
(xiv) 5,11 (xv) 1,11 (xvi) 4,14 (xvii) 4,11

The first point has been plotted for you.

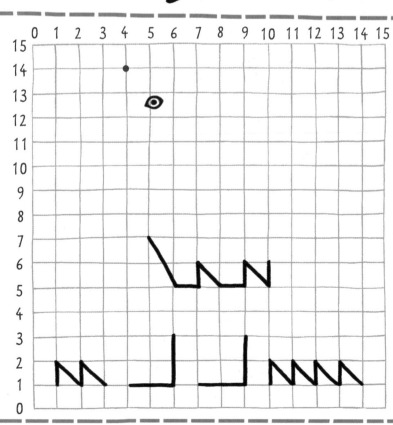

WEATHER WATCHING

You don't always need to hear the forecast to know what the weather's going to be like. Just take a look around you...

SIGNS OF FINE, SUNNY WEATHER

Fluffy, white clouds high in the sky

Birds flying high

Smoke rising steadily from a barbecue

SIGNS OF WET, STORMY WEATHER

Dark clouds clustering together

Birds diving and flying low

LEAFY MAZE

Find a way through this grid, moving from one leaf to the next. You can move up, down, left or right but you must step on the leaves in this order: fir, oak, maple, fir, oak, maple...

FIR   OAK   MAPLE

START

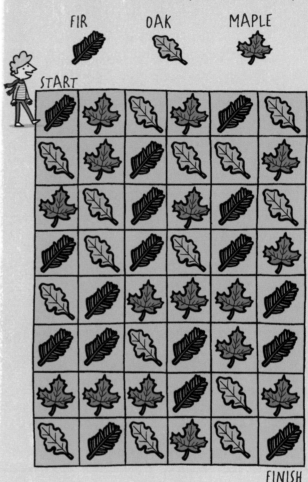

FINISH

FISHING-BY-NUMBERS

Follow the instructions to find out which fish the boy catches, then continue the fishing line to this fish.

CROSS OUT:

☆ odd numbers

☆ single-digit numbers

☆ the number of years in a decade

☆ the number of sides three dice have

☆ the number of legs two spiders have

Flying high

This plane is flying high in the clouds. Draw passengers in the windows.

Cloud words

Can you unscramble all the jumbled-up words floating in this cloud?

LPAEN

NDWI

....

....

NILGFY   YSK   DIRB

....

Bird pairs
Spot the identical birds. Which one doesn't have a partner?

Quick quiz

1. Some planes can travel faster than the speed of sound. True or false?

2. The very first hot-air balloon passengers were a sheep, a duck and a rooster. True or false?

Doodle more birds in the sky.

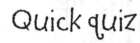

3. Planes can't fly at night. True or false?

4. It is dangerous for hot-air balloons to fly in the rain. True or false?

HA HA HA!
Q: What do clouds want to be when they grow up?

A. Thunderstorms.

5. Some clouds are so thick you could lie on them. True or false?

PICNIC TIME

It's a lovely day for a picnic and these hungry bears have been enjoying the food! Can you spot ten differences between the two pictures?

SUMMER FIZZ

To make a summer fizz, you'll need:

Squeeze us!

2 lemons   50g (2oz) raspberries

100g (4oz) caster sugar   1 litre (1¾ pints) sparkling water

1. Mash the raspberries with the sugar until the mixture is smooth.

2. Add the lemon juice and two tablespoons of cold tap water. Stir until the sugar dissolves.

3. Sieve the mixture, using a spoon to push all the liquid through.

Serve with ice cubes.

4. Then, add the sparkling water.

PICNIC LEADER

You could play this fun game at a picnic.
First, choose someone to be the leader.

1. Stand behind the leader, and copy what he does.

2. The leader keeps doing actions, until only one other person's still playing.

Leader

If you get it wrong, you're out.

She's out.   He's the new leader.

HA HA HA!

Q: How can you tell if an elephant has been at your picnic?

A: There are footprints in the chocolate cake.

SUPER SANDWICHES

To make one perfect picnic sandwich, this chef used two pieces of bread, one slice of cheese, two pieces of lettuce, two tomato slices and two cucumber slices. How many more complete sandwiches can he make from these ingredients?

Answer: ....

Doodle more bees in the swarm.

An ant has sneaked onto these picnic pages – can you find it?

Tropical sands

These golden sands need covering with lots of stickers – buckets and spades, crabs, sandcastles, starfish, shells, and animals having fun in the sun.

Crazy crab race

Some crabs can only walk sideways – how fast can you move that way?

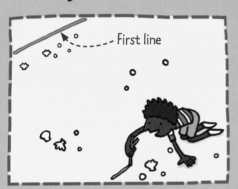  

1. Draw two lines on a sandy beach, about twenty paces apart.

2. Everyone gets on their hands and feet, behind the first line. Someone shouts 'Go!'

3. They all race sideways to the other line – the first to cross it is the winner.

Stylish sunglasses

These people all need to wear sunglasses when they go to the beach – doodle some on for them.

Flowers

Hawaiian leis (flower necklaces) come in lots of bright colours. Each of these has a pattern – can you fill in the remaining flowers to finish the patterns?

AT THE MOVIES
In the audience

There are lots of things to spot in this audience. Colour in all the things you can find on the list, doodle more people in the empty seats, then colour in the rest of the picture.

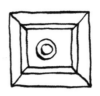

☆ a boy spilling popcorn
☆ three pairs of glasses
☆ two people wearing ties
☆ a banana
☆ six people wearing hats
☆ a pair of identical twins

Movie poster

This poster is advertising the next summer blockbuster. Fill in each section that has a black dot in it, until the picture is revealed.

Popcorn

Doodle arms, legs and faces on the popcorn kernels.

Movie director

Choose someone to be the movie 'director'. Everyone else is an 'actor'.

1. The director tells the actors to do an action.

Anyone who doesn't do the action straightaway is out.

2. The director tells the actors to do more actions. If he doesn't start an instruction with 'The director says...' and someone does the action, they are out.

3. The last person still in the game is the winner, and becomes the new director.

Snack sudoku

Draw pictures of these four movie snacks on this grid. Every row and column must have one picture of each kind of snack.

DID YOU KNOW?
Some movies are so long that it would take days to watch them!

75

AMAZING ADVENTURE

On these pages, write what happens when you go on an incredible imaginary adventure.
The story's been started for you, and there are lots of words and pictures to inspire you:

On the day of my adventure, I awoke, yawned and stretched, as I always did. Suddenly, I heard a loud...

AIRCRAFT

TREKKING

CREAK!

SPOOKY HOUSE

TOTAL DARKNESS

gloomy

SPACE ROCKET

hazardous

zOOM!

OUTER SPACE

WHIZZ!

shooting star

wOw!

ASTOUNDING

SWORD FIGHT

CLANG!

LOST CITY

mysterious

DING!

fast cars

murky

VROOM!

deep oceans

PLOP!

SCUBA DIVING

Breathtaking

BOOM! whOOSH! HISS! perilous EXCITING

SKYDIVING. FREEZING COLD AWE-INSPIRING SEARING HEAT DARING sinister

THUD!

sparkling jewels

CRUMBLING CASTLE

CLANK!

TERRIFYING

INCREDIBLE

COURAGE

RESCUE

dark cave

BEEP BEEP BEEP

VOLCANO exhilarating poison FANTASTIC perplexing

ROAR! THRILLING pouring rain PING!

CITYSCAPE

Look closely at this view of a busy city and see if you can spot and circle:

☆ three green cars

☆ nine skyscrapers with triangular roofs

☆ two clock faces

☆ ten yellow taxis

☆ three green houses in a row

☆ a helicopter

☆ six pale yellow houses with red roofs

Paper city

To make a city panorama picture, you will need:

Old magazines and newspapers

Glue   Scissors

Black pen

1. Draw a black line for the street.

2. Cut skyscraper shapes out of paper. Glue them on in a row.

3. Add windows with a black pen.

Try cutting out some window shapes from magazines too.

Which way?

Look at the map, then put the directions in the correct order for someone walking from the train station to the gallery.

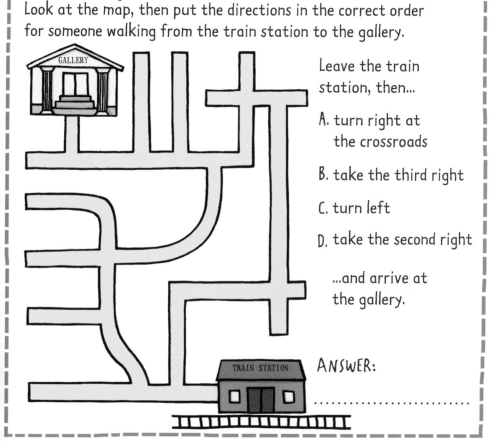

GALLERY

TRAIN STATION

Leave the train station, then...

A. turn right at the crossroads

B. take the third right

C. turn left

D. take the second right

...and arrive at the gallery.

ANSWER:

....

Bus route

Can you guide this bus through the grid of letters? Move up, down, left or right, one letter at a time, to trace a continuous path through four places a bus might pass in the city.

E	R	T	H	L	→ END
P	C	A	E	A
A	R	C	D	R
U	R	S	Y	K
A	A	N	M	S
T	S	T	U	E
R	E	M	U	S

START →

SAFARI PARK

DRAW A RHINO

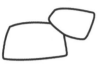

Draw a head and body.

Add four legs and a tail.

Give it two horns and a face.

Fill in the rhino.

𝒟oodle
more rhinos.

DID YOU KNOW?
The biggest rhinos' horns are longer than 1m (3 feet).

MEERKAT MUDDLE

Can you help my brother find his way out of the burrow?

DID YOU KNOW?
Meerkats can close their ears, to keep out soil when they're burrowing.

GIRAFFE GRID

Can you find these three squares in this picture?

EXAMPLE:

 = B3   =   =   =

GREEDY PELICAN

How many fish is this pelican about to eat?

DID YOU KNOW?
Pelicans can scoop up lots of fish in one go.

DID YOU KNOW?
A giraffe's neck can be as tall as a person.

DID YOU KNOW?
Galapagos tortoises are very heavy. They can weigh more than five people.

TORTOISE TOWER

Add patterns to these tortoises' shells

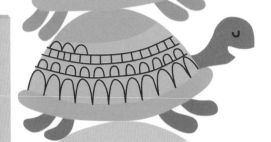

WORLD DESTINATIONS

These postcards have been sent from around the world. Can you solve the puzzles on them?

MYSTERY POSTCARD

I'm on holiday – can you crack the code to find out where I am? Love Bella x

```
F Y T G L E   Y   U M L B C P D S J
_ _ V _ G _   _   W _ _ D E _ F U
R G K C   G L   A Y J G D M P L G Y
_ _ M _   _ N   C _ L I F _ _ N I
-  G R ' Q   F M R !
-  I _ ' S   H _ T !
```

A=	B=	C=	D=	E=
F=	G=	H=	I=	J=
K=	L=	M=	N=	
O=	P=	Q=	R=	
S=	T=	U=	V=	
W=	X=	Y=	Z=	

Can you find a little bird hiding on one of the stamps on this page? Fill it in, then fill in the other stamps, too.

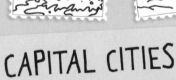

SILENT STATUES

Huge stone figures like these stand on Easter Island in the Pacific Ocean. See if you can spot the odd one out.

CAPITAL CITIES

Which of these trails do I need to follow, to fly from London to Moscow? Thanks, and see you soon, Alex

On this poster, a boy has come to visit his friend, but which way does he need to go?

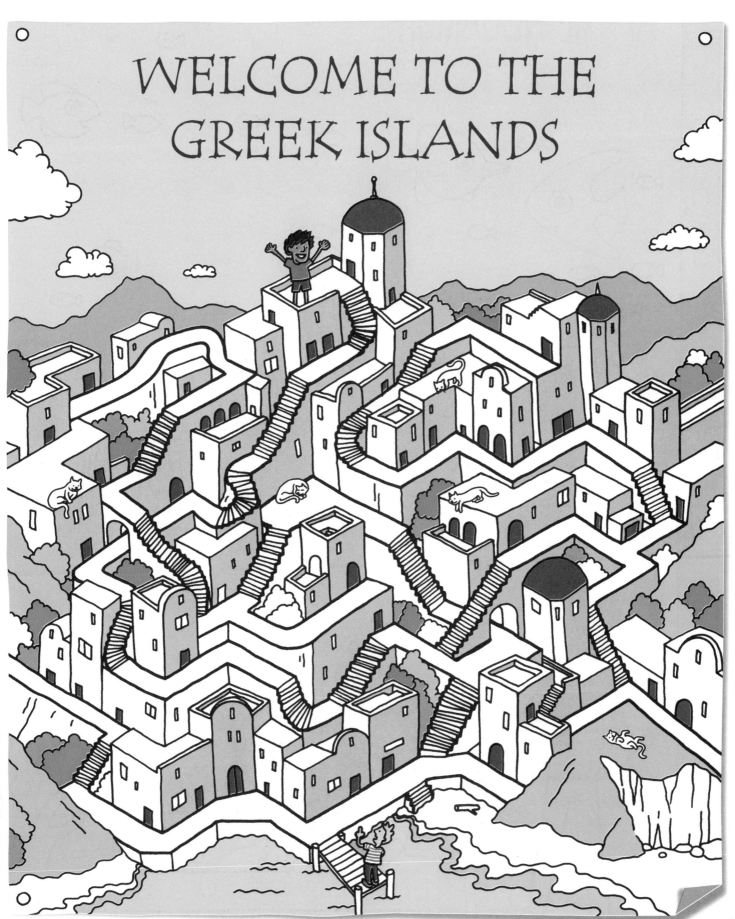

WELCOME TO THE GREEK ISLANDS

AT THE AQUARIUM

Join up the numbered fishes from 1 to 297 to reveal the giant sea creature hiding in this tank.

Fill in the fish with bright pens.

Draw squiggly lines on the fish, to give them scales.

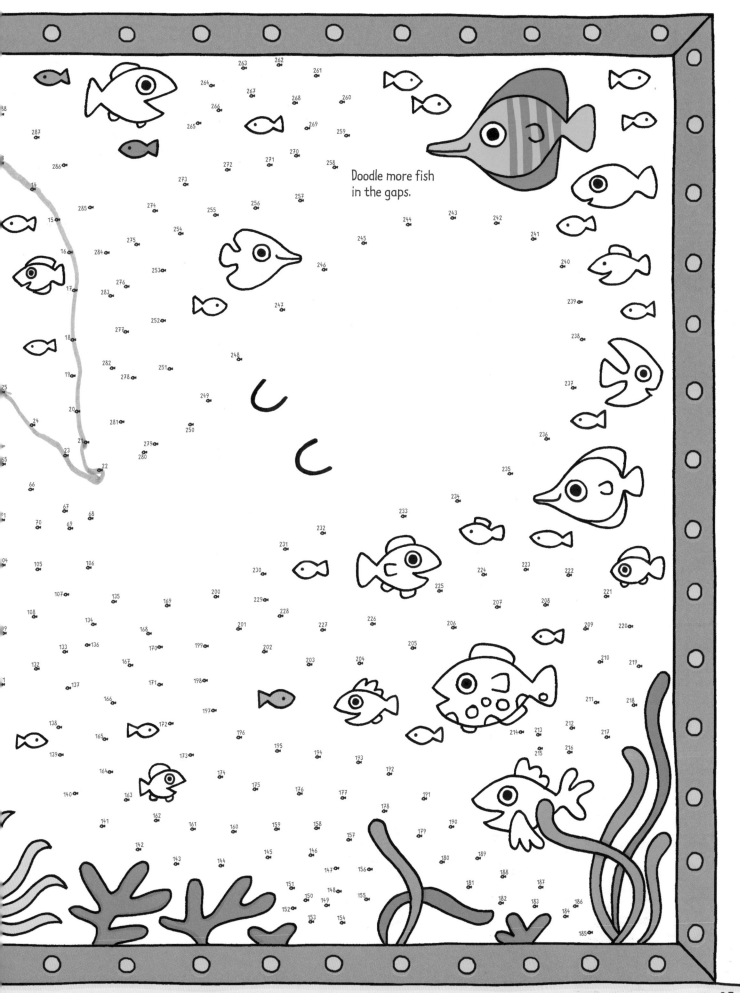

Doodle more fish
in the gaps.

Ski Resort

Doodle
lots of people snowboarding and skiing, then fill in the picture.

Follow the steps at the bottom to find out how to draw snowboarders and skiers.

Add more bubble cars along the cables.

DRAW A SNOWBOARDER...

1. Draw a head, body, arms and legs.

2. Then, add a snowboard.

...AND A SKIER

1. Draw a head, body, arms and legs.

2. Add two skis and two ski poles.

Draw tracks behind the skiers.

DID YOU KNOW?

Not all skiing goes downhill – cross country skiing can be done in any snow-covered place, even if it's quite flat! It's very energetic as skiers use their arms, legs, skis and poles to move along.

IN THE JUNGLE

Animal forest

There are lots of animals hiding in these rainforest trees. Look out for frogs, snakes, monkeys, and tarantulas, as you colour in the picture.

Jungle quiz

1. Some kinds of tarantulas eat birds. True or false?

2. What do colobus monkeys do when they're happy?
   a) Fly   b) Swim   c) Burp

3. Hummingbirds make an ear-splitting noise when they hover in the air. True or false?

4. The biggest rainforest in the world is the:
   a) Amazon   b) Congo   c) Daintree

5. Fruit bats prefer eating bugs to eating fruit. True or false?

6. Rafflesia plants smell like:
   a) Roses   b) Rotting meat   c) Garlic

7. Some of the biggest trees in rainforests are over 1,000 years old. True or false?

8. The biggest jungle cats are:
   a) Jaguars   b) Leopards   c) Tigers

Cliff climber

This climber is leaving the jungle. Can you find a safe route for him to the top of the cliff?

Slippery snakes

These snakes are in a tangle. Fill in each snake with a different pattern.

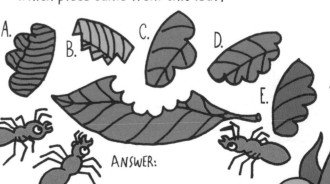

Leafcutters

Leafcutter ants use their jaws to cut up leaves. Which piece came from this leaf?

A.   B.   C.   D.   E.

ANSWER:

....

A LAND OF ICE AND FIRE

PUFFIN PAIRS

Which puffin doesn't have a matching twin?

SNOWY SIGNS

There are some amazing geological sights to see, but the signs pointing the way to them are partly covered with snow. Can you complete the words?

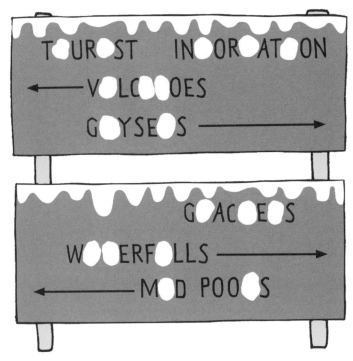

T U R ST   IN OR AT ON
← V LC OES
G YSE S →

G AC E S
W ERF LLS →
← M D POO S

ICY ADVENTURE

Adam needs to get home, collecting as few points as possible. There are lots of obstacles in his way, each with a different number of points. Add up the points along each route, to find out which is the best way for him to go.

OBSTACLES

MOUNTAINS = 1

SPOUTING GEYSER = 3

ICY GLACIER = 2

BOILING HOT LAVA = 4

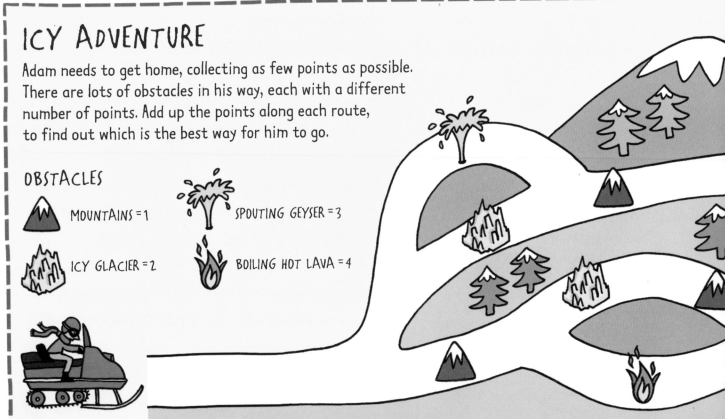

WHALE-WATCHING

The people on this ship are on a trip to see whales.
How many whales are there?

Number of whales: ....

ERUPTION?

Fill in the missing numbers, to see if the volcano erupts.

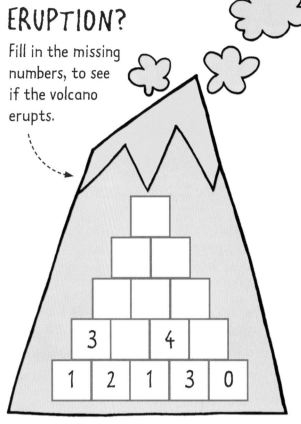

3		4	
1	2	1	3	0

Each number is the sum of the two numbers below it. If the number at the top is over 25, the volcano erupts. Does it?

YES/NO

Do any sums here: - - - - ➤

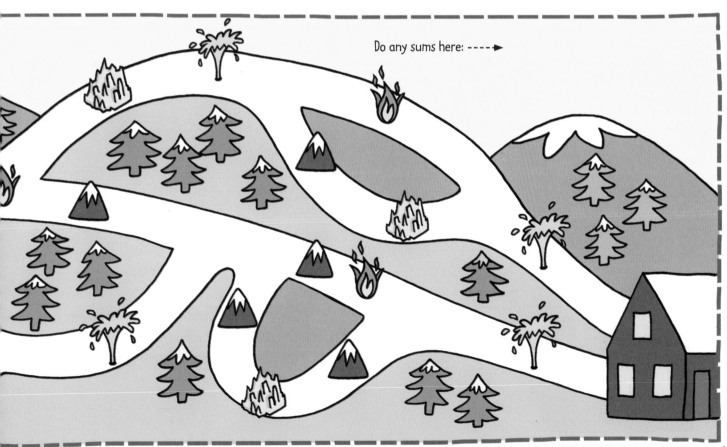

Answers and solutions

2-3 READY TO GO

SHADOW SHAPES:

CLICKING CAMERAS:

ONE MORE THING...:

4-5 ALL ABOARD!

PORTHOLE PUZZLE:
33 rooms will have people staying in them.

LINING UP:

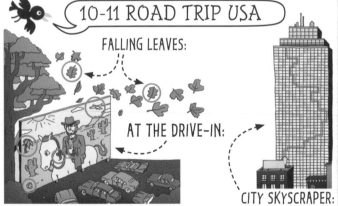

6-7 BEACH FUN

OFF FOR A SWIM:

TANGLED STRINGS:
A is flying kite 4,
B is flying kite 2,
C is flying kite 3,
D is flying kite 1.

BEACH RACE: Runner C wins, with 15 points.

10-11 ROAD TRIP USA

FALLING LEAVES:

AT THE DRIVE-IN:

CITY SKYSCRAPER:

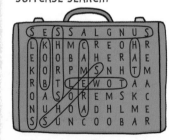

12-13 DEPARTURES AND ARRIVALS

SUITCASE SEARCH:

DESTINATION UNKNOWN:

ROME,

PARIS,

TOKYO,

NEW YORK,

BEIJING.

FIND THE CASE:

PASSPORT CONTROL:

MR. M. BIRD
02/03/1983
975831

MR. M. BIRD
03/02/1983
975831

14-15 ON BOARD SHIP

DESTINATION DILEMMA:
THE SHIP IS SAILING TO JAMAICA.

PUSH THE PUCKS:
Draw one puck on section -10, two pucks on section 7 and one puck on section 8.

18-19 ISLAND-HOPPING

VILLAGE VISIT:

Men in white hats:
People with dogs:
Man taking a photograph:
Birds:
Cats:
Boys eating ice cream:
Artist painting a picture:

FISHING PUZZLE:
Juan caught 26 small fish, Noah caught 19 medium-sized fish, and Alex caught 6 big fish.

ISLAND NAMES:
IABL = Bali, ZIABI = Ibiza,
ETREC = Crete, BRODSABA = Barbados

20-21 AT THE CARNIVAL

FANTASTIC FIREWORKS:

CARNIVAL PARADE:

Jugglers: ◯ Blue lanterns: ◯
Red noses: ◯ Hat with flower: ◯

22-23 HOLIDAY HOTEL

WHAT'S DIFFERENT?:

BATHROOM SUDOKU:

DINING ROOM DILEMMA: Seven

MENU CODE: THERE IS A FLY IN THE SOUP.

ELEVATOR RACE: A

24-25 SUMMER GARDEN

LOST IN A MAZE:

MAKE THE BED:

BUG SEARCH:

1 caterpillar: ◯ 4 spiders: ◯
11 beetles: ◯ 5 butterflies: ◯
  5 bees: ◯

26-27 GALLERY GAZING

PICTURE IMPERFECT:

SQUARED: 20 squares

28-29 THEME PARK FUN

SUPER SPINNER:

WILD WATER:
The person in the green ring will get the wettest.

BRILLIANT BALLOONS: Balloon 3 is going to pop.

WIN A PRIZE:

32-33 HOLIDAYING AT HOME

FRIENDS' VISIT:
Lucy and Armand are coming to visit.

SPOT THE SPOONS:

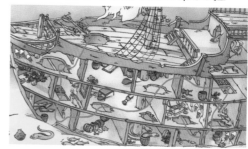

BARBECUE PRANKS:

34-35 DIVING FOR TREASURE

36-37 ELEPHANTS AND SPICES

BUSY VILLAGE:
6 houses: ◯
2 elephants: ◯
4 cows: ◯
5 cats: ◯
8 dogs: ◯
2 bicycles: ◯

These are the answers to the sums:

[A] Houses 6 ÷ Elephants 2 = 3
[B] Cows 4 x Cats 5 = 20
[C] Dogs 8 ÷ Bicycles 2 = 4
Answer [B] 20 ÷ Answer [C] 4 = 5
+ Answer [A] 3 = 8 - Cows 4 = TOTAL 4

FIND THE GEM:

SPICE SHOP:

⧄ ⧄ △ ○ ⟨ △ • ⧠ = turmeric
⧠ △ • ▽ ▽ △ ◌ = chilli
⧠ ⧄ ○ • ⧠ = cumin
⧠ • ⧄⧄ | ○ \ ⧠ = cinnamon
▽ • ⧄⧠ ▽ ⟨ △ = ginger

42-43 ON THE SLOPES

WHICH WAY DOWN?:

NAME EVERY MOUNTAIN:
EVEREST, FUJI, McKINLEY, KILIMANJARO.

ODD SKIER OUT:

SORT THE SKIS:

SNOWED OUT:
12 − 5 + 3 = 10,
14 − 2 − 1 = 11,
90 − 40 + 30 = 80,
7 + 3 + 2 − 4 = 8.

44-45 IN THE MUSEUM

Lost umbrella:
Orange cat:
Snakes:
Red handbag:
Cameras:

Mobile phones:
Museum leaflets:
Someone asleep:
People wearing hats:

46-47 CASTLE DAY OUT

ARMOURY: B and D are symmetrical.

LIBRARY:

BANQUETING HALL:
Draw two candles on the last stand, and leave the other empty. (Pattern: −4, +2, −4, +2, −4, +2)

1=○ 2=○ 3=○

COURTYARD:

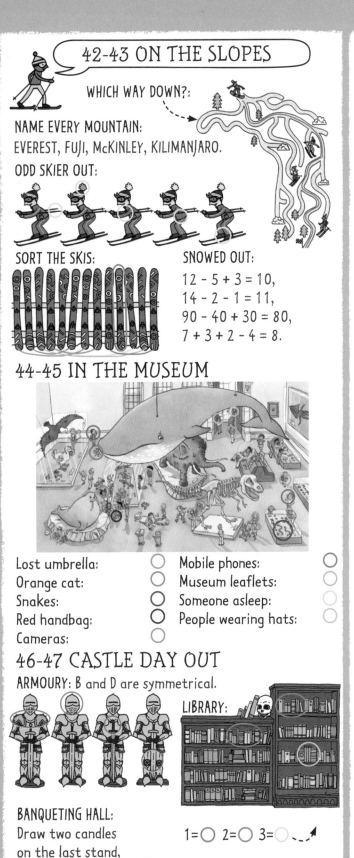

50-51 CAMPING OUT

PITCH THE TENTS:
The tents should be in this order around the camp fire, from left to right: blue, orange, red, green, yellow.

MARSHMALLOW SEQUENCE:
3, 6, 9, 12 (Sequence: +3, +3, +3)
2, 4, 8, 16 (Sequence: ×2, ×2, ×2)
35, 28, 21, 14, 7 (Sequence: −7, −7, −7, −7)

PACK THE BACKPACK: CLOTHES, FLASK, TORCH, WATER BOTTLE, SLEEPING BAG

52-53 DESERT DAY OUT

HOT HIKERS:

TRUE OR FALSE?:
1. False, 2. True,
3. True, 4. False,
5. True

OUCH!:
The cowboy landed on cacti B, D and E, getting 3 spines from B (which has 17 spines left), 1 spine from D (19 spines), and 3 spines from E (17 spines).

ROCKY WORDS:

CANYON CLIMB:

HUNGRY ARMADILLO: Trail C.

54-55 BOREDOM BUSTERS

CODE-NAMED CREATURES:
1. C. COCKROACH
2. B. MOUSE
3. A. RHINOCEROS

PATTERN PROBLEM:

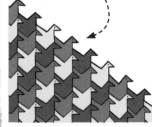

COLOUR SQUARES:
Red = 2, Yellow = 4, Blue = 6
A. 22, B. 14, C. 14 , D. 22

FROM ABOVE:
1. Someone wearing a big hat and frying an egg
2. Someone wearing a yellow helmet on a bike
3. Someone holding an umbrella and standing in a puddle

GUESS HOW?: The boy gives his seventh friend the box with the seventh chocolate left in it.

58-59 JAPANESE JOURNEY

SIGHTSEEING: 4C

LUCKY CATS: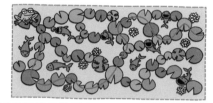

SUSHI SEQUENCE: B.   **COUNT THE CHERRY BLOSSOMS:** 55

SUPER SUSHI: **LILY POND:**

60-61 OUT OF THIS WORLD

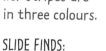

SPACE TOURISTS: **ROCKET SHIP:**

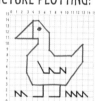

TRUE OR FALSE?: True

SPACE BUGGIES:
You can only make two whole buggies, so no, there won't be enough buggies for them all.

STAR PUZZLE:
'STAR' appears five times.

CODED MESSAGE:
EARTH LOOKS GREAT FROM HERE! (This is how the code works: 1=A, 2=B, 3=C, and so on.)

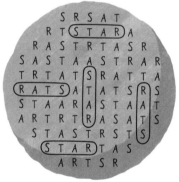

62-63 CHILLING OUT

SNOW MYSTERY: C.

ISLAND CRUISE: The ship visits four islands in total, and its destination is Egg Island.

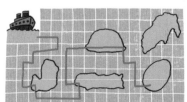

FLAG-FINDER:
Sweden = D.
Finland = A.
Norway = C.
Denmark = B.

64-65 WATER PARK

WHICH IS FASTEST?: B.   **SUPER SLIDES:** D.

SWIMMERS:
Her stripes are in three colours.

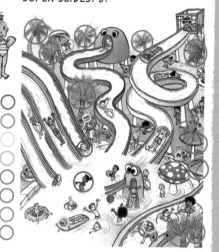

SLIDE FINDS:
Yellow swimsuits: ○
Dropped ice cream: ○
Sunglasses: ○
Lady in a red hat: ○
Palm trees: ○
Sun umbrellas: ○
Brown bird: ○
Red flowers: ○

66-67 IN THE WILDS

TRACKING DOWN:
DEER
PONY
DUCK
HERON
BEAR
SQUIRREL

LEAFY MAZE:

PICTURE PLOTTING:

FISHING-BY-NUMBERS:
Fish 24

68-69 UP IN THE AIR

CLOUD WORDS:
NDWI = WIND, LPAEN = PLANE, NILGFY = FLYING, YSK = SKY, DIRB = BIRD

BIRD PAIRS: **QUICK QUIZ:**
1. True 2. True 3. False
4. True 5. False

70-71 PICNIC TIME

TEDDY BEARS' PICNIC: **SUPER SANDWICHES:** 6

The ant is here:

72-73 TROPICAL SANDS

FLOWERS:

74-75 AT THE MOVIES

IN THE AUDIENCE:

A boy spilling popcorn: ○	A banana: ○
Pairs of glasses: ○	People wearing hats: ○
People wearing ties: ○	Identical twins: ○

SNACK SUDOKU:

78-79 CITYSCAPE

SPOTTING CITY:

WHICH WAY?: D., A., C., B.

BUS ROUTE:

RESTAURANT, MUSEUM, SKYSCRAPER, CATHEDRAL

Three green cars: ○	A helicopter: ○
Two clock faces: ○	Six pale yellow houses with red roofs: ○
Ten yellow taxis: ○	
Three green houses in a row: ○	Nine skyscrapers with triangular roofs: ○

80-81 SAFARI PARK

MEERKAT MUDDLE:

GIRAFFE GRID:

=E9

=G3

=G11

GREEDY PELICAN: 16

82-83 WORLD DESTINATIONS

MYSTERY POSTCARD:

Having a wonderful time in California – it's hot! (This is how the code works: A=C, B=D, C=E, and so on.)

STAMPS:

The little bird is on the statue's shoulder.

SILENT STATUES:

The second statue from the left is the odd one out – it's smiling.

GORGEOUS GREECE:

CAPITAL CITIES: Trail B.

88-89 IN THE JUNGLE

CLIFF CLIMBER:

JUNGLE QUIZ:

1. True 2. c) Burp
3. False 4. a) Amazon
5. False 6. b) Rotting meat
7. True 8. c) Tigers

LEAFCUTTERS: D.

90-91 A LAND OF ICE AND FIRE

PUFFIN PAIRS:

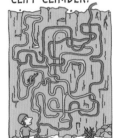

SNOWY SIGNS:

TOURIST INFORMATION / VOLCANOES/ GEYSERS / GLACIERS / WATERFALLS/ MUD POOLS

WHALE-WATCHING:
There are 11 whales.

ERUPTION?:
Yes, the volcano does erupt.

	27		
	13	14	
6	7	7	
3	3	4	3
1	2	1	3	0

ICY ADVENTURE:

This route gives him the fewest points: 14.

First published in 2012 by Usborne Publishing Ltd., Usborne House, 83-85 Saffron Hill, London EC1N 8RT, England. www.usborne.com © 2012 Usborne Publishing Ltd. The name Usborne and the devices are Trade Marks of Usborne Publishing Ltd. All rights reserved. No part of this publication may be reproduced, stored in a retrieval system or transmitted in any form or by any means, electronic, mechanical, photocopying, recording or otherwise without the prior permission of the publisher. UKE.